PAPER INNOVATIONS

handmade paper and handmade objects of cut, folded and molded paper

Library of Congress Catalog No. 85-063043
Published by Mingei International
Museum of World Folk Art

University Towne Centre, 4405 La Jolla Village Drive
(mailing address: P.O. Box 553, La Jolla, CA 92038)

6   ISBN# 0-914155-04-0

A DOCUMENTARY PUBLICATION OF MINGEI INTERNATIONAL MUSEUM'S
EXHIBITION—*PAPER INNOVATIONS*
CURATED BY MARTHA LONGENECKER
CIRCULATED BY THE ART MUSEUM ASSOCIATION OF AMERICA.

THE EXHIBITION WAS MADE POSSIBLE IN PART BY
MERVYN'S
THE DIRECTOR'S CIRCLE

THE PUBLICATION WAS MADE POSSIBLE BY
CHAMPION INTERNATIONAL CORPORATION
THE KNIGHT AID FUND
ANNA SAULSBERY
THE SEYMOUR E. CLONICK MEMORIAL FUND

TIGER—FOLDED PAPER

3"H x 7"L x 2½"W

JAPAN, Contemporary

Collection of Mingei International

Photograph by Allyson P. Kneib

CONTENTS

COVER—FOLDED PAPER PULL TOY—INDIA (Contemporary)

PAGE 2—TEXTURE PAPER TIED IN PREPARATION FOR TIE DYING

MINGEI INTERNATIONAL GRATEFULLY THANKS THE SPONSORS AND ALL THOSE WHO HAVE GENEROUSLY CONTRIBUTED, IN MANY SPECIAL WAYS, TO THE EXHIBITION AND DOCUMENTARY PUBLICATION, *PAPER INNOVATIONS*. THESE INCLUDE MUSEUM STAFF, DOCENT AND VOLUNTEER COUNCILS, AND MEMBERS.

INTRODUCTION
Martha W. Longenecker, Founding President and Director

PAPER INNOVATIONS: Handmade Paper and Handmade Objects of Cut, Folded and Molded Paper will have fulfilled its purpose if you, the reader, find it helps deepen your sensitivity and understanding of the nature and use of this remarkable, man-made material.

The exhibition was inspired by the contemporary resurgence of interest in the art of paper making, and is designed to give a glimpse of our rich international heritage in the innovative making of paper and art objects of paper.

A major gift to our museum of an international paper collection and library on paper, donated by author Florence Temko, was the initiating impetus for MINGEI INTERNATIONAL to organize and present this exhibition.

Plans for the exhibition were further stimulated by seeing the extraordinary paper collection of the Paper Museum, *Yamane Washi Shiryokan*, of Tottori, Japan, and the willingness of its director, Mr. Shio, to lend choice pieces.

The exhibition might also be entitled *PAPER CYCLE*. Throughout the entire development of paper since its origin in China over two thousand years ago, plant fibers of old paper and cloth have been used over and over again, to create new paper of great variety, beauty and quality.

Paper that has disintegrated with the passing of time, or been discarded, may again be recycled and have a new life in a fresh new piece of paper, or in a delightful paper maché object.

The fibers within a sheet of paper in our hand or within the objects of the exhibition may well have been a part of other uses of the past.

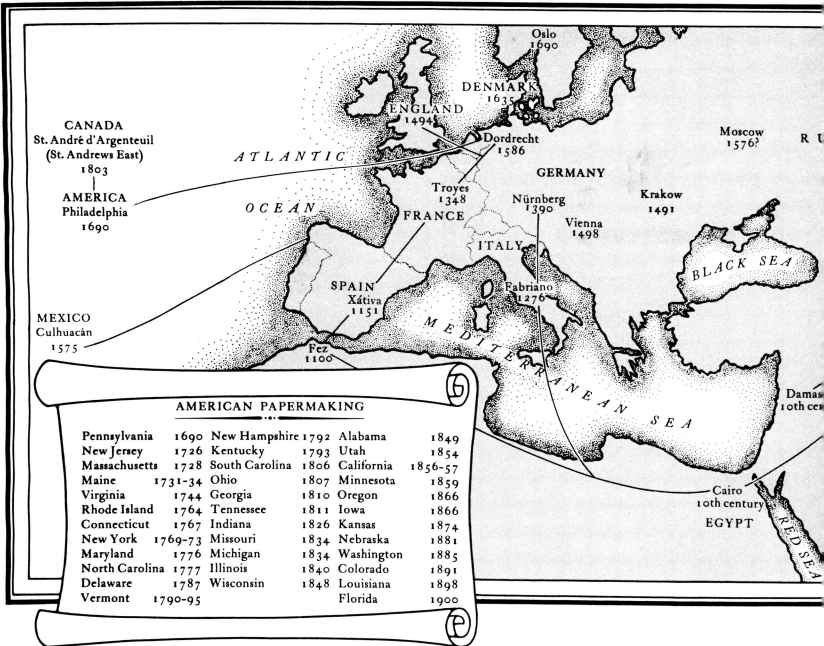

CANADA
St. André d'Argenteuil
(St. Andrews East)
1803

AMERICA
Philadelphia
1690

MEXICO
Culhuacán
1575

ATLANTIC

OCEAN

Oslo
1690

DENMARK
1635

ENGLAND
1494

Dordrecht
1586

GERMANY

Moscow
1576?

R U

Troyes
1348

FRANCE

Nürnberg
1390

Krakow
1491

Vienna
1498

ITALY

SPAIN
Xátiva
1151

Fabriano
1276

Fez
1100

MEDITERRANEAN SEA

BLACK SEA

Damas
10th cer

Cairo
10th century

EGYPT

RED SEA

AMERICAN PAPERMAKING

Pennsylvania	1690	New Hampshire	1792	Alabama	1849
New Jersey	1726	Kentucky	1793	Utah	1854
Massachusetts	1728	South Carolina	1806	California	1856–57
Maine	1731–34	Ohio	1807	Minnesota	1859
Virginia	1744	Georgia	1810	Oregon	1866
Rhode Island	1764	Tennessee	1811	Iowa	1866
Connecticut	1767	Indiana	1826	Kansas	1874
New York	1769–73	Missouri	1834	Nebraska	1881
Maryland	1776	Michigan	1834	Washington	1885
North Carolina	1777	Illinois	1840	Colorado	1891
Delaware	1787	Wisconsin	1848	Louisiana	1898
Vermont	1790–95			Florida	1900

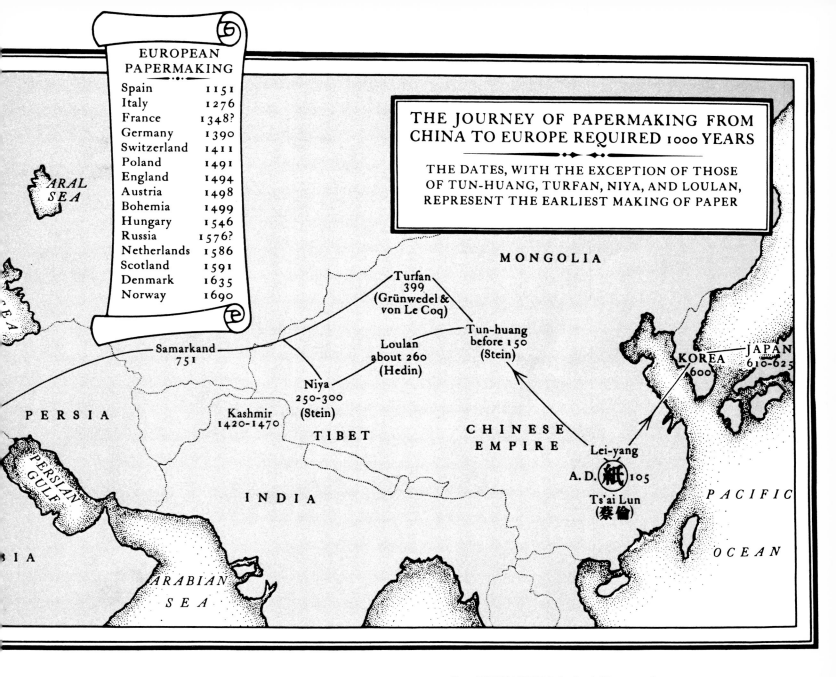

THE JOURNEY OF PAPERMAKING FROM
CHINA TO EUROPE REQUIRED 1000 YEARS

THE DATES, WITH THE EXCEPTION OF THOSE
OF TUN-HUANG, TURFAN, NIYA, AND LOULAN,
REPRESENT THE EARLIEST MAKING OF PAPER

ARAL
SEA

MONGOLIA

Turfan
399
(Grünwedel &
von Le Coq)

Tun-huang
before 150
(Stein)

Samarkand
751

Loulan
about 260
(Hedin)

KOREA
600

JAPAN
610-625

Niya
250-300
(Stein)

PERSIA

Kashmir
1420-1470

TIBET

CHINESE
EMPIRE

Lei-yang

PERSIAN
GULF

INDIA

A.D. 紙 105
Ts'ai Lun
(蔡倫)

PACIFIC

ARABIAN
SEA

OCEAN

From PAPER MAKING, by David Hunter   Courtesy of Dover Publications, 1978

THE DAWNING OF PAPER MAKING IN CHINA

Susan Olsen

A plant structure is broken apart and the elements are recombined into a new form. This is the essence of the papermaking process. How did humans ever conceive of the idea of doing this?

Let's imagine ourselves thousands of years ago in the land of China, standing with friends on a river bank. We watch the surging current as it breaks apart plant structures and carries them to be screened between reeds and branches...or to be left interlaced on the porous earth as the water subsides.

Now and again we visit a certain pond and notice that plants decompose as they soak in the still water over a period of time. The fibers remain intact as the material that bonds them dissolves or ferments.

People began to put to use these recycling processes that they observed occurring spontaneously in nature. Since ancient times in China it was common to recycle old rags of linen and hemp. People would beat them and break them down, swish them around in water and pour them over a screen to dry. Later this mat of floss would be used to stuff quilts. The routine was documented in the first century A.D., Imperial annals, the *Shou wen chieh-tzu*—the first comprehensive Chinese dictionary. The mat of refuse fibers was called *chih* (pronounced *tchrer*).

Thousands of years ago people hit upon a key alchemical reaction—the effect of spontaneous fermentation could be simulated in an accelerated fashion by cooking the plant structure in a solution of water and plant ashes (alkali). People utilized this discovery to secure cellulose fibers which are the raw material for textiles.

In China, the silk culture harnessed the process in this way: cocoons were simmered in grass ash solution to dissolve the glue that bonded the shimmering filament. Then the cocoons were placed in a basket that was immersed in a stream while the contents were gently beaten with a stick to encourage the loosening of the filament.

14

Papermaking in China
from a coloured drawing by an unknown native artist
circa, 1800

Victoria and Albert Museum

Now the filament could be unravelled and wound in one continuous strand—the best one and a half kilometers long! But if a cocoon had been spun imperfectly, the strand would fragment.

Now we imagine the scene of a woman lifting the basket out of the stream. She removes the flawless cocoons, and the fragmented strands remain interlaced at the bottom of the basket. Later, when it dries, she peels off the fine glistening sheet. This *mat of refuse silk* was also called *chih.*

Towards the end of the first millenium B.C., people made *chih* with the intention of forming flat, thin sheets. Refuse silk, rags and fish nets were the fiber sources. At first the sheets were used as a wrapping material; later they began to serve as a writing surface.

At the dawn of the new millenium there was a growing demand for *chih* which was paralleled by the need for more source materials; silk was expensive and there were just so many rags and fish nets to recycle. People were beginning to process plant structures themselves by boiling in an alkaline solution and beating to obtain the needed cellulose. Among the first source plants were hemp, flax and jute.

The Empress T'eng of Han Dynasty sensed the social and economic relevance of "chih" and writing. The new communications media was to develop during the next few centuries at a quantum leap pace—a phenomenon that was not to be equaled until the current dynamic emergence of electronic communications.

In 105 A.D. the empress sanctioned T'sai Lun, a court official who was a great innovator in papermaking, to announce officially the invention of paper under Han auspices.

Chih then took on a new meaning: *paper*. The essential papermaking process was defined in the literature of the times as:
tsoa, peel; *tao*, macerate; *chao*, pour over screen.

"The paper is the painting" is the name Susan Olsen gives for the art form she practices. At present she works in her studio in Los Angeles and is establishing a special learning center in Kauai.

BURIAL GARMENT

___"H x 39¼"W

CHINA, 20TH C.

Collection of Mingei International

Photograph by Allyson P. Kneib

17

FUNERARY PAPERS

14¾"H x 13¼"W

BURIAL GARMENT

54¼"H

CHINA, 20TH C.

Collection of Mingei International

Photograph by Allyson P. Kneib

JAPANESE PAPER MAKING

Sukey Hughes

Paper in Japan has long been both the humblest and most sacred of substances. From its manufacture into clothing and accessories, into bedding and umbrellas and toys, into lanterns and doors and handkerchiefs, into luggage and fans and banners—to its ritual use as folded white *gohei* strips sanctifying sacred areas, and as paper charms and sutras, paper has been a prime material and medium of expression for the Japanese psyche. It has touched all of life in Japan. And the Japanese, knowing with what labor and time it has been made, have always treated their handmade papers with deference, if not reverence.

The Japanese have made paper by hand for over 1200 years. These handmade papers, known as *washi,* are among the strongest and most beautiful in the world—resilient, lustrous, warm ingenuous, and the best of them, nearly ageless. Hundreds of varieties are made in hundreds of patterns, colors and surfaces, from the delicate-looking "lace" papers to sturdy art papers and woven paper clothing.

The Japanese learned how to make paper in 610 A.D. from the Korean monk-physician, Doncho. Doncho taught the techniques first developed in China, that is, taking rags and certain plants, boiling and macerating the fibers, placing the fibers in a vat with water, and drawing a flexible bamboo screen, held firmly in a mold, through the vat solution, picking up fibers as the water drained through the screen. Immediately the Japanese realized the significance of what they had been taught. Experiments with new materials and methods began, and soon the Japanese had added their own innovations to the papermaking process. First, they started making papers solely from vegetable fiber; second, they added plant mucilage to the vat, enabling them to manufacture thin, smooth sheets. Moreover, the added mucilage evidently corrected a certain brittleness and poor sheet formation characteristic of these earliest papers.

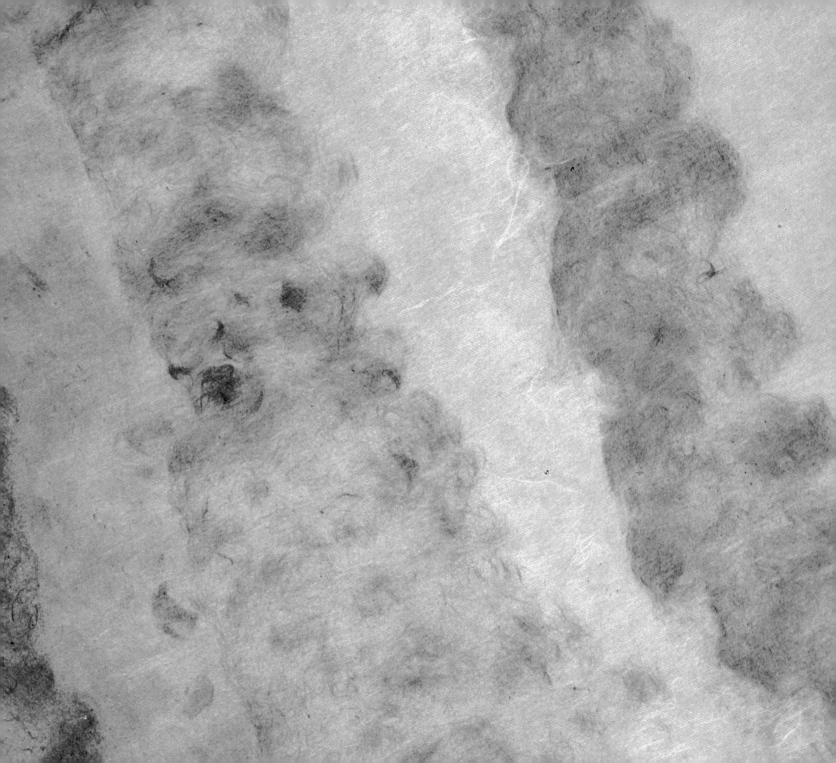

Eishiro Abe making paper.

    a. composing the wet fibers on a bamboo screen.

    b. transferring a fresh sheet of wet paper from the screen and stacking on top of other wet sheets.

    c. Lifting a finished sheet of paper from the stack after the excess water has been pressed out.

Photographs by Kazuhiko Ohori

HANDMADE PAPER (Section)   (see preceeding page)

16½″ x 53″   (Full sheet size)   by the late Eishiro Abe, A Living Treasure of Japan

JAPAN, 20TH C.

Collection of Mingei International

Photograph by Jim Coit

These innovations in materials also gave rise to a totally new manner of forming sheets. This is called *nagashi-zuki,* literally "casting-the-liquid-off papermaking." It consists of casting off excess pulp from the screen during the sieving process, and enabled the papermaker to produce exquisitely thin sheets, and to make thicker sheets remarkably smooth and even in formation. The mucilage so important to this technique is added to the vat just before sheet formation. It is usually made from the crushed root of the rose mallow, *tororo-aoi.* This clear, viscous liquid thickens the pulp solution, and so retards the time it takes for the water to drain through the screen. This is to the papermaker's advantage; there is time to manipulate the solution on the screen the desired way, creating a certain horizontal or vertical grain or a mixture of horizontal and vertical. The papermaker can also regulate the amount of fiber he wishes to remain on the screen, tossing off any excess amount or any unwanted "wild" fibers.

The earliest Japanese papers are thought to have been made of hemp, the inner bark of the now infamous *Cannabis sativa*, and later of *gampi*, a cousin to our daphne. Experiments in applying other barks to paper manufacture were encouraged by Prince Shotoku (574-622), notably with *kozu*, a generic term for several varieties of mulberries. Today mulberry bark is the most commonly used papermaking fiber in Japan. A third shrub, *mitsumata*, was discovered as a paper-making fiber in the 16th century. Today the three major sources of fiber for paper are *kozo, mitsumata,* and *gampi,* in that order. *Kozo* is long-fibered, masculine, tough, sinewy, very white, and capable of making a wide range of different papers from the finest, sheerest tissue to heavy woodblock paper. *Gampi,* known as the king of the papermaking fibers, is also very tough, although the fibers are thinner and finer. Of the Thymelaeaceae family, *gampi* contains a bitter chemical repugnant to insects, which helps it endure for centuries. *Gampi* can produce hard-surfaced sheets as translucent as tracing paper. The third fiber in the papermak-

WOODBLOCK PRINT ON HANDMADE PAPER

"Flower Hunters" by Shiko Munakata   53½ "H x 64½ "W

JAPAN, 20TH C.

Collection of the Japan Society—Japan House Gallery, New York City
Photograph by Allyson P. Kneib

ing triad is *mitsumata*. Belonging to the same family as *gampi*, it also contains the same insect-repelling chemical. *Mitsumata* has the shortest fibers of the three, is soft, absorbent and of reddish-beige hue and has a less aggressive character than the other fibers. Japan also uses bamboo, rice straw, hemp, cotton and wood pulp to make handmade paper; rice straw and wood pulp in particular are used because they are cheap and convenient, although they mostly detract rather than add to *washi*'s beauty and durability.

Making paper the traditional Japanese way is dependent upon the land's bestowal of two essentials, good water and cold climate. The country is plentiful in both. Water is essential to every phase of papermaking, and the best paper demands that the water be pure, cold and moving. In humid, mountainous Japan, a wealth of rivers and streams has encouraged through the centuries the formation of papermaking villages. Deep artesian wells and fresh mountain streams fed by melting snows have provided Japan with excellent water free of minerals and impurities detrimental to fine papermaking. This quality water gives paper a lucidity it could not otherwise achieve, and its freedom from iron and manganese helps ensure the long life of the paper.

Cold helps paper become fresh-looking, crisp and strong. Cold temperatures throughout the papermaking process prevent bacteria from growing and assist the mucilage in taking effect in the vat; moreover, cold tightens and contracts the bark fibers, encouraging their strength and long life. Paper made in cold has a crisp rattle and feel to it, feeling substantial. Not surprisingly, then, the best paper is made in winter.

Although some villages in Japan are devoted year-long to papermaking, by and large papermaking is a winter activity undertaken by farmers to supplement their farming income. Between the end of November and the winter solstice, the autumn

FAN WITH STENCIL—DYED DESIGN

16″H   by the late Keisuke Serizama, Living treasure of Japan

JAPAN, 20TH C.

Collection of Mingei International

kozo is harvested. When they have shed their leaves, *kozo* trees two years of age or older are cut down, trimmed of their smaller branches, bound into bundles and taken to be steamed. Whole trees are never cut down; by taking only the stalks cut to about six inches from the ground, a whole new series of stalks grow back in their place again in a year. This is papermaking with ecology in mind.

It is the inner, white bark that is sought in Japanese papermaking, and to strip it from the woody tree core usually requires steaming. Either a giant metal closet with fire beneath it, or a very large metal pot are the steamers. Shoots are placed upright in the container with some water, covered or closed tightly, and a fire ignited underneath. Within three to twelve hours the steaming is completed. The hot shoots are removed by the farmers and placed on straw mats where the whole family, young and old, joins in stripping the bark from the cores, laughing, singing, teasing and gossiping. Then the farmer dries the bark over poles in the sun for one to three days, after which it is bound and stored. In this state the bark can keep for years in storage.

As winter advances, the dry, hard bark is taken from storage and soaked for a few days in the river. At this point the worker may tread upon it right in the river, releasing flakes of outer bark. Then the worker places the semi-cleaned bark on a board or holds it in the lap over a scraping stump and scrapes it to remove any remaining black bark as well as scars, insect holes and other imperfections in the white flesh. Though painstaking and tedious, this cleaning contributes greatly to the fineness and whiteness of the finished sheets. At this point the papermaker places the bark in bundles in the river and weights the bundles with stones; the combined effects of sun and cold water improve the bark's whiteness and strength. In colder areas the papermaker may lay the bark over the snow. River-bleaching and snow-bleaching are effective ways of whitening the paper naturally. Chemical bleaches

HAND BAG — HAND SEWED KAMIKO PAPER
6"H   Tanned with Persimmon Juice   by Hiroko Noguchi
JAPAN, Contemporary

Photograph by Jim Coit

weaken the paper fibers and slowly eat away at it over the years. Such chemical bleaching is found in Japan today more than ever, unfortunately; Papermakers are aware of its disastrous effects, and the best papermakers avoid it entirely.

To soften and begin breaking down the fiber, the bark needs to be boiled in an alkali solution. Again the bark is soaked in water, then placed in a large cauldron of boiling water. Either lye from wood ash or soda ash is then added to the pot. The worker cooks the bark in this manner for anywhere from one to twelve hours, the time depending on the age of the fiber, the quantity of it and the strength of the alkali solution. A few papermakers resort to using caustic soda to speed up the cook time and give the fiber a certain finish; however, this also weakens the fibers. The finest papermakers agree that a minimum of treatment and chemicals produce the strongest and most beautiful papers. When the bark can easily be torn apart, the cooking is finished. The bark is rinsed thoroughly, and taken away for more cleaning. In the most tedious process of all, *chiri-tori*, older workers float the broken-down fiber in baskets placed in small canals of water, and pick out any remaining dark fibers. This extra cleaning is for the preparation of the very whitest, finest paper.

The papermaker places the melon-sized balls of cleaned fiber on a wooden table or smooth granite stone and beat it with hardwood rods or mallets for the final breakdown. This hand beating undoubtedly produces the most beautiful fiber, and although it is fortunately to be seen more and more as the appreciation for it increases and people are willing to pay for the added labor, still, most fiber in Japan today is beaten by mechanical stampers or with a Hollander beater. The stamper is the preferable method of the two, imitating the hand beating by a crushing and mashing action that helps the fibrillation of fibers; the Hollander produces a more homogenized fiber that is not quite as strong. The monotonous and rhythmic sounds

CEREMONIAL UMBRELLA
98″H x 83″ Diameter
JAPAN, Contemporary

Photograph by Jim Coit

WOODEN LANTERN
HANDMADE PAPER

14 ¼ "H x 10⅝"W x 9⅝"D

JAPAN, 20TH C.

Collection of Martha Longeneck

Photograph by Allyson P. Kneib

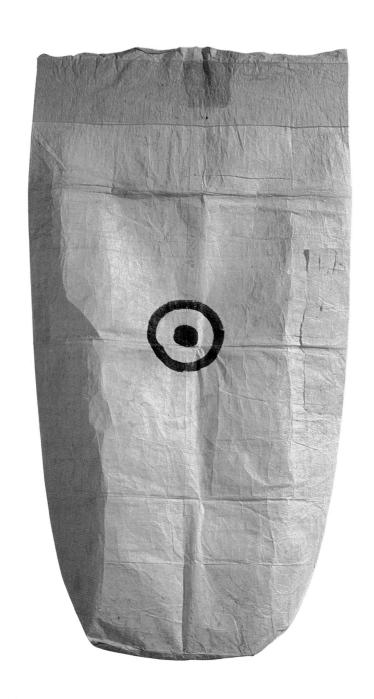

BAG FOR STORING SILK COCOONS

Gampilo Paper made from Kozo fiber

JAPAN, c. 1800

Collection of Margaret Sahlstrand

Photograph by Jim Coit

of hand beating gave rise years ago to many papermaking songs, and poems as well. About a century ago women often had to beat the fiber all day and continue beating all night too as market day approached and papermaking work reached a crescendo of industry:

> The papermaking girls of Kuzu are worse off
>   than beggars.
> Don't beggars sleep at night, and in the daytime too?

To prepare the stock to make paper, the pulp is stirred into a large vat of water at about a one to two ratio. The papermaker agitates the mixture to blend it with a large comb-like rake. Then she squeezes a porous bag full of the viscous mucilage, called *neri*, over the vat and mixes the solution again with a bamboo stick. The papermaker fits a rectangular and flexible screen, made of the finest bamboo splints, into a wooden mold, and lowers the screen-mold rapidly into the vat, scooping up some of the milky solution. Through carefully executed shaking and tossing motions, she causes the fibers to cross and cohere across the screen as the water drains away. She repeats the process of *nagashi-zuki*, as described earlier, until she has attained the desired sheet thickness. She removes the dripping screen, wet sheet attached to it, from the mold and carefully places it, paper-side down, on a board covered with wet cloth. Pulling the screen away, the wet sheet remains on the stack. She builds up a post of sheets in this manner, placing each newly-made sheet (a process called "couching") on top of the last. The Japanese make no use of interleaving felts to separate the sheets, although sometimes a reed or length of string is placed over each sheet as it is stacked to make separation easier. An experienced papermaker can make 200 or more large sheets in a day. Because the large molds are frequently divided down the middle, a papermaker can pull two half-size sheets at once, thus producing 400 or more sheets in a day.

DARUMA—PAPIER MACHÉ

5½"H x 3½" Diameter

JAPAN, 20TH C.

Collection of Mingei International

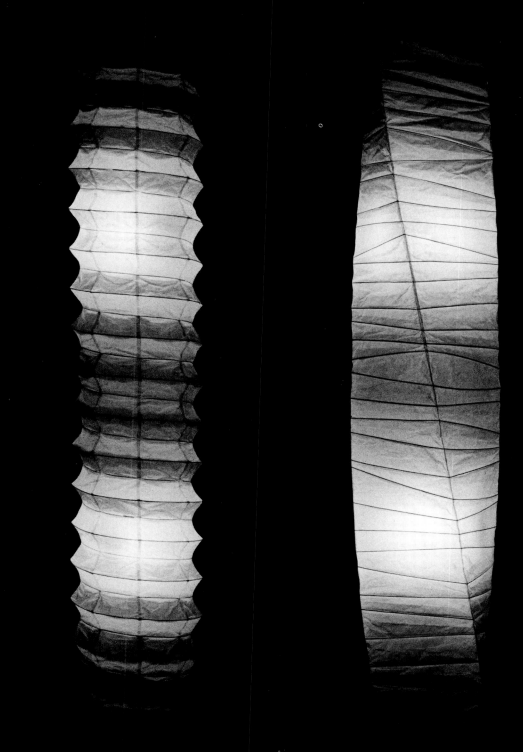

ANTERNS OF HANDMADE PAPER
signed by Isamu Noguchi

PAN, Contemporary

llection of Mingei International
otograph by Michio Noguchi

AI-BOMORI'' — FISH LANTERN

per on Bamboo Frame   24½"H x 12"W x 24"L

PAN, Contemporary

llection of Amaury Saint-Gilles
otograph by Jim Coit

Pressing the wet post of sheets is an important step in the papermaking process, requiring skill in judgment and patience. Pressing the sheets too quickly causes them to adhere to one another. If pressed too long or too hard, the paper will be too dry to mount on the drying boards. If pressed too little or lightly, the paper remains too weak and wet to handle without tearing. After the stack of sheets rests over-night the workers place it in a screw press or hydraulic press and apply pressure slowly over a period of hours. Amazingly, the sheets can be separated after pressing; this almost magical act is possible because of the great internal strength of each sheet, a strength enhanced by the use of the mucilage and hemicelluloses released in the beating stage.

One by one the papermaker carefully parts the sheets from the pile and places each on a smooth wood board, brushing it down with a soft, wide horsehair brush. He carries the boards of paper into the sun, if it is a fine day, where they dry quickly. Increasingly papermakers use steam-heated metal indoor dryers, which are fast and avoid bad-weather problems, but many purists complain that paper dried in this manner tends to shrink or warp later with humidity changes.

Of all the myriad articles the Japanese have made out of paper, of special note in this exhibition is the manufacture of woven paper clothing, called *shifu*, literally "paper clothes." This sophisticated textile is made when a cut sheet of paper is rolled on a stone to make the strips threadlike, then woven on a loom into cloth. It may also be spun on a spinning wheel prior to weaving. The cloth is then cut and sewn into kimonos, jackets and various purses and accessories. While *shifu*'s origins are not well known, references to it appeared first around 1650. Early *shifu* production was in Miyagi and Fukushima Prefectures. It may have originated when a local Shiroishi samuari named Sanada created a way to make extremely tough cord out of twisted paper for armor bindings — reportedly no sword could cut through it. Soon this cord was woven into sandals and worn by firemen who walked them through water before entering fire areas. Eventually the finer paper cords were woven into cloth, a perfect material for hot weather for, like linen, it is lightweight, cool and airy. Surprisingly, *shifu* can be washed, but not roughly.

"GINGASA" — PAPIER MACHÉ HAT

11"H

"GINGASA" — HAT

10½"H   Woven Paper Fibers

JAPAN, 19TH C.

Collection by Yamane Washi Shiryokan, Tottori, Japan

A kind of crude *shifu* with paper a both warp and weft was once worn by peasants for underwear as well as used for pillows, futon, coats and mosquito netting. The most refined *shifu* of all is *kinujifu* with paper weft and silk warp, difficult to make and enjoyed by the wealthy for summer wear. Today *shifu* manufacture enjoys a mild revival in several places in Japan.

The Japanese have preserved the best of the ancient paper-making techniques with an almost fanatic integrity, handing them down from mother to daughter and father to son, generation upon generation. These traditions combine heavy labor in processing the fiber with refined craftsmanship when at the paper vat. Working close to nature, in rivers and meadows, the traditional ways offered the papermakers affection for their craft while it demanded care in the rituals of work, permitting no shortcuts and no waste, neither of time nor materials. These are the only "secrets" of Japanese papermaking, the magic behind paper of incredible beauty, strength and endurance.

Sukey Hughes of Santa Barbara, California, is a papermaker and paper historian who also teaches the craft. She is the author of *Washi: The World of Japanese Paper.*

FARMER'S JACKET—PAPER WEFT, COTTON WARP

42"L x 54½"

JAPAN, 20TH C.

Collection of Yamane Washi Shiryakan, Tottori, Japan

JAPANESE PAPER TEXTILES

Margaret Sahlstrand

Papermaking in Japan rapidly reached a highly developed state after its introduction from Korea in 610 A.D. One important use was in the production of fabric for clothing. The first paper robes were made by a monk named Shoku in 988, who, as the story is told, used the backs of old sutras, or scriptures of Buddha. This nonwoven paper cloth—formed of layers of paper glued one to another—was called kamiko (from the words *kami,* "paper," and *koromo,* "a priest's robe"). Kamiko served to make a warm garment that could be repaired with paste and more paper when torn and which was destroyed when soiled. Today the monks of Todai-ji Temple still dress in these austere robes during the Omizutori ceremony in March in the city of Nara.

Kamiko soon became popular among the poor since paper was abundant, inexpensive, and very warm in winter. The paper was made strong and waterproof, as it still is today, by treating it with *konnyaku,* a colorless, liquid vegetable starch, which was worked into the paper with the hands. After treatment, the sheets of paper were glued together to form bolts of paper cloth, which could be cut and stitched into clothing in the traditional manner.

Many household items were made of this paper cloth—blankets, pillows, and linings for conventional garments—yet the kamiko garment proved by far the most popular use of the cloth. Just as its popularity increased, so too did the garments status; and by the Edo Period (1615-1868) the wealthy and the nobility frequently sported elegantly dyed, stenciled, and embroidered examples of kamiko both for daily wear and for tea ceremonies.

Around 1638 a second type of paper cloth made its first appearance in formal records. Called *shifu* (from *shi,* "paper," and *fu,* "cloth"), this woven paper fabric had similarly humble origins. Since the winter months precluded working

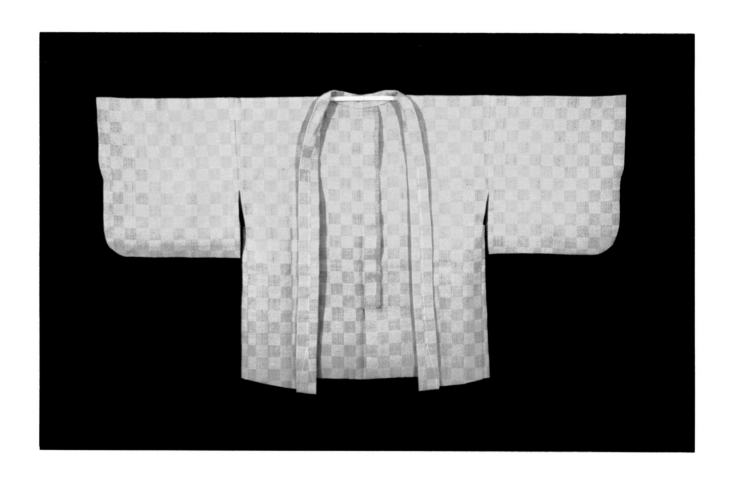

WOMAN'S SHORT COAT — PAPER THREAD WEFT AND SILK WARP

30"H   (detail of weave on page 45)

JAPAN, Contemporary

by Sadako Sakurai

43

KIMONO—Paper thread weft and silk wrap
By Sadako Sakurai
63½″H x 48″W
JAPAN, C.

44

in the fields, farmers turned to making paper in this season. Soon they joined league with peasant weavers who developed a way to cut a sheet of paper into thread and spin, dye, and weave the thread. The lightweight garments they in turn produced were durable and washable and in time became the favored summer dress of the poor.

As the weavers gradually refined their techniques, word of the fabric's increasing beauty reached the nobility. Under the patronage of the local ruling lord, the fabric became one of great elegance, upon which was lavished the same care and complex dyeing techniques that were used for silk. The high regard for shifu—bolts of which were once offered in tribute by the Lord of Shiroishi to the Tokugawa Shogun—waned during the 19th century industrialization of Japan when inexpensive machine-made cloth became readily available, and by the early 1920s neither shifu nor kamiko was being produced.

In 1940, however, the Local Crafts Institute was founded in Shiroishi by three men—Chutaro Sato, Tadao Endo and Nobumitso Katakura—whose express mission was the revival of shifu and kamiko. Through the efforts of Mr. Katakura, in 1955 the government designated shifu an Intangible Cultural Property, a distinction akin to the honored title of Living National Treasure, bestowed by the Emperor on selected craftsmen.

Seiki Kikuchi is a contemporary paper maker who makes *shifugami,* a paper produced especially for shifu. His papers are used by Mrs. Sadako Sakurai of Mito, a modern master who produces elegant work in the spirit of the Edo Period. Her fabric for purses, made of cotton warp-and-paper weft is soft yet strong enough to withstand constant use.

In addition to the cotton warp-and-paper weft shifu, the most common form of shifu, there are other forms as well: *kinujifu,* made with a silk warp and paper weft; *morojifu,* woven with both a paper warp and weft; *asajifu,* which has a linen warp and paper weft; and *chirimenjifu,* a creped fabric found only in old shifu in museums and private collections.

Sadako Sakurai opening out a cut sheet of paper during the pre-spinning process. After
this step, it is spun on the wheel.   (see following page)   47

Shifugami is unique among handmade papers. Since the advent of inexpensive machine-made cloth, this paper was not in great demand and hence not commonly produced in Japan. When Sadako Sakurai could find no suitable paper for her shifu work, she contacted papermaker Kikuchi to ask if he would consider making shifugami for her work. The paper he now makes represents years of collaboration with Sadako Sakurai, to whom he recently presented four new papers for testing for the finest thread she makes.

The production of shifugami is very demanding. As with all paper, the principal ingredients of shifugami are fiber and water, both carefully selected. Kikuchi uses the kozo fiber from the paper mulberry shrub of his native Ibaraki Prefecture, known throughout Japan for its long, strong fiber and beautiful color. He makes the paper in winter when the water from the mountain behind his home is cold and pure. Carefully prepared during each step of cooking and cleaning, the cleaned fiber is beaten in water to separate it into the individual fibers. These are then mixed in a vat with more water and a small amount of vegetable mucilage, *tororo-aoi,* which keeps the particles in suspension and facilitates catching the fiber on the mold's surface in a very thin layer.

During the sheet-forming process the paper mold is shaken only vertically, aligning the long fibers in one direction. This vertical alignment provides the inner structural strength the paper needs when cut into fine strips for making thread. Since new paper is too brittle for making thread, a year's supply is made in advance so that it may age properly.

Mrs. Sadako Sakurai has developed her own methods of spinning paper thread, based on experiment, written accounts of shifu production, and study of the noted shifu collection of Mr. Katakura, Japan's foremost scholar and collector of shifu. She begins making thread by cutting the paper into fine strips no more than 2 mm. wide. Care is taken not to cut the top or bottom edges of the sheet. Next, the paper is dampened slightly and the entire sheet rolled by hand on a porous cement block. After the sheet has been thus rolled five times, it is straightened out with a sharp tug so that the cut strips lie parallel. This is done

200 times until the paper is prespun, or begins to take a twist. The process leaves Sakurai's hands raw since it takes one to two months of work to prepare the thread for weaving.

In the next step the edge of the paper sheet is torn through. By alternately tearing the top and bottom edge, the sheet can be opened into one continuous strip of thread about 260 meters long. The sheets are then joined as they are spun on the wheel. When the spinning is finished, the thread is stabilized by steaming, which is necessary to prevent the finished fabric from coming apart when washed. Once spun, the paper thread is woven on a loom to form textiles of traditional kimono and obi lengths and widths.

Margaret Sahlstrand is a fiber artist, papermaker, also a professor at Central Washington Unversity, Ellensburg, Washington and founder of ICOSA studio and papermill.

WEDDING DUCK — WOVEN PAPER

COVERED BOX — WOVEN PAPER

5"H x 5½" Diameter

KOREA, 19TH C.

Collection of Mr. and Mrs. George Brosius

Photograph by Carlos Richardson

50

51

STATIONARY BOX — ''FUMI BAKO''

5″H x 17″W x 10″D

KOREA, 19TH C.

Collection of Yamane Washi Shiryokan, Tottori, Japan

PAPER CHEST WITH LACQUER FINISH

62⅔"H x 29¼"W x 17¾"D   Skeleton wood frame

KOREA, YI DYNASTY (1392-1910)

Collection of Yamane Washi Shiryokan, Tottori, Japan

PAPER CHEST WITH LACQUER FINISH

39"H x 39"W x 17"D   Skeleton wood frame

KOREA, YI DYNASTY (1392-1910)

Collection of Yamane Washi Shiryokan, Tottori, Japan

PAPER CASE— "TATOH"

9½ ″L x 6½ ″W

JAPAN, 19TH C.

Collection by Yamane Washi Shiryokan, Tottori, Japan

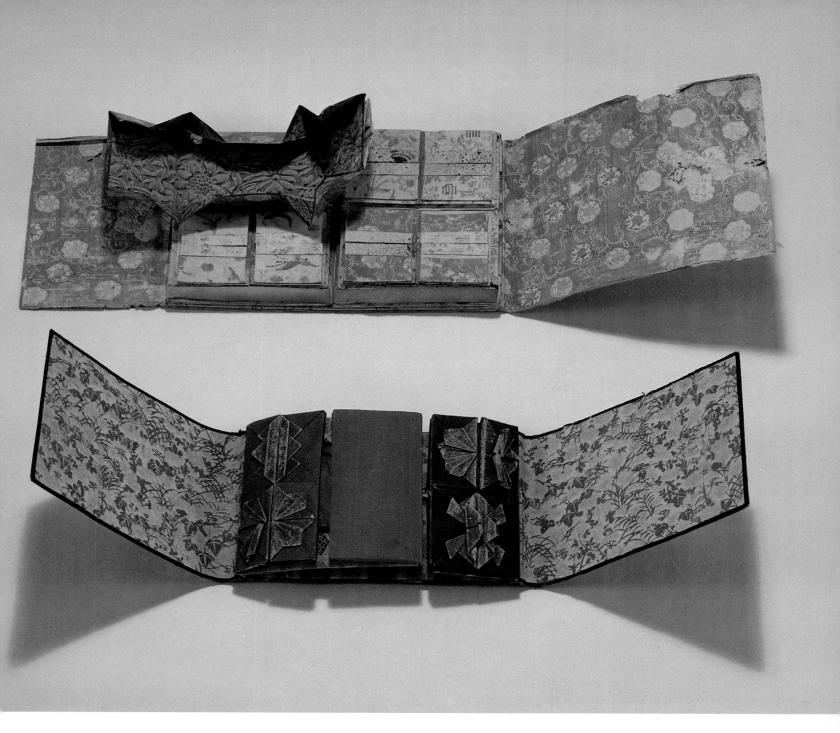

THE HISTORY OF PAPER FOLDING

Florence Temko

Paperfolding is an ancient art, yet its history is not well documented, which can be attributed to the fact paper is perishable. Scholars conjecture paper was folded in China, perhaps before the sixth century.

Paperfolding or *Zhe Zhi* in Mandarin and *Chip Chee* in Cantonese was gaining popularity until Liberation in 1949, when other priorities prevailed. In keeping with the traditional ancestor worship, Chinese burn paper replicas of worldly goods at funerals and annual cermonies to provide the deceased with comfort in the afterworld. These re-creations may include clothing, farm animals, treasure chests, luxury cars and refrigerators. Most are made of colorful paper cut and pasted over bamboo strips, but gold nuggets and other items are purely folded. This religious practice was banned in the People's Republic of China after Liberation, but continues to some extent in Chinese communities elsewhere. In Hong Kong and Singapore paper houses, cars and a chest filled with gold nuggets are common at many Chinese funerals.

At the present time paperfolding is not widespread in the Chinese mainland except as an occasional means of providing toys for children.

Paperfolding is most highly developed in Japan where it has become a popular folk craft called origami, with its origins in Shinto and Zen Buddhist philosophies.

Origami is a Japanese word for folding pieces of paper into objects without cutting or pasting.

It is believed paperfolding was imported to Japan and Korea when the process of making paper was introduced from China in the sixth century. The earliest reference to paperfolding occurs in a manuscript of the Edo Period (1614-1868), which mentions a box of pre-folded origami figures, implying such collections were available for sale as long ago as 1728.

60

BROTHER LION DANCER

3 ¾ "H x 9 ¾ "W   (One of pair)

Paper Fold by Mrs. Toshie Takahama

JAPAN 20TH C.

Photograph by Allyson P. Kneib

Paper folded in prescribed forms called *Noshi* were traditionally used as gift wrappers symbolizing good wishes. At the present time such stylized designs in simplified forms are still attached to gifts, like small gift cards, but are little known to Westerners, except as forerunners of contemporary paperfolding.

Children learn origami at home and in elementary schools and as a result many Japanese remember how to fold a crane and one or two other things. The crane is a traditional Japanese symbol of good fortune and longevity and has now also become the symbol of peace.

Origami has developed into a more elaborate adult art form with exhibitions held from time to time. Akira Yoshisawa is considered the most prominent artist. Since 1966 Yoshisawa has traveled to over thirty countries in order to spread the art of origami and in 1983 was decorated by the Emperor for his efforts to help friendly relations among nations of the world. Before portraying any animal Yoshisawa studies its anatomy and habits for long periods of time, in order to be able to imbue his creation with its characteristics and soul. His originals are quite spectacular.

Paperfolding is becoming better known everywhere, folded ornaments having even found their way onto the Christmas tree at the Presidential White House in Washington. Paperfolders are always busy at Christmas time, because paper ornaments are charming and easy to make. Every December a 60-foot tree decorated with hundreds of animals is a regular feature at the American Museum of Natural History in New York City, becoming more elaborate each year. And each Christmas other trees appear at many other locations.

Leonardo da Vinci is considered the earliest experimenter with paperfolding and other famous folders include Samuel Johnson, Lewis Carroll, Unamuno, Houdini and convicted banker Michael Sidona. During the 18th and 19th centuries it was customary in Germany to fold baptisimal certificates and other religious documents in decorative ways and at the end of the 19th century the German educator Froebel instituted kindergarten schooling for children and included paperfolding in the curriculum.

ORIGAMI BY AKIRA YOSHISAWA

one swan   5″ x 7″x 1½″

JAPAN, Contemporary

In the United States, England, Spain, Italy, France and other Western countries, the craft has attracted many followers. While most people enjoy folding a square of paper into a bird or a box as a form of amusement, some skilled enthusiasts create works of art which are shown in mixed media exhibitions in museums and art galleries. The exhibits vary from miniature insects no larger than half an inch to giant abstracts four feet across, pure white or exuberantly colored. Some forms may have only a few creases while others may have as many as 250.

Making paper by hand has emerged as a new art form during the 1970's, and papermakers are just beginning to discover that traditional paperfolding steps can add a new dimension to their work.

From: "CHINESE DUCKS AND 55 OTHER THINGS TO FOLD WITH PAPER"
© Florence Temko
Publisher China Books & Periodicals, S.F.

THE BREMEN TOWN MUSICIANS

20¾"H x 6½"W x 3"D Origami by Florence Temko

UNITED STATES, Contemporary

Collection of Mingei International

Photograph by Allyson P. Kneib

PAPER FOLD

by Florence Temko

UNITED STATES, Contemporary

Collection of Mingei International

Photograph by Allyson P. Kneib

PULL TOY — FOLDED PAPER

3½"H x 27"L x 3½"W

INDIA, Contemporary

Collection of Mingei International

68   Photograph by Jim Coit

"BAPTISM" PAPERCUT

18″H x 75″L

POLAND, 1960

Collection of Fred and Barbara Meiers

Photograph by Jim Coit

PAPERCUT (above)

41"Long

CHINA, 20TH C.

Collection of Mingei International

Photograph by Allyson P. Kneib

TWO OF THE EARLIEST SURVIVING PAPERCUTS

CHINA, 5TH C.   (following pages 75 and 77)   73

CHINESE PAPERCUTS

Florence Temko

The Chinese specialty of cutting paper pictures with the simplest means has provided the world with some delightful small works of art. They are produced by two distinct methods, depending on whether they are cut with scissors or knives.

Chinese papercutters have developed a system used nowhere else. Their scissors weave a continuous line in and around the paper. Eyes and other features which lie within the interior of the design are reached by incising a snip to reach the area and then cutting away a circle of whatever shape is appropriate. Traditional Chinese scissors have large, almost oval handles and short blades which are always kept sharp. Cuts begin at the cross of the scissors and continue along the blades as far as necessary. The tips are used only for delicate trimming.

Scissor cutting is suitable for making one or two pieces at a time and is the method preferred by master artisans and housewives who craft for home consumption.

Traditionally Chinese cuts are made from flat paper, and only recently have I seen a symmetrical scissor cut made from a folded piece of paper. I attribute this to artistic interchanges which are now taking place between China and the West, where cutting into folded paper is more prevalent. The weight of paper used can be compared to typing paper or giftwrap.

Knife cutting is the most widely practiced method and permits producing large quantities. A whole stack of paper can be cut at one time, yet the artisan is able to incise minutest details, whether these be facial features or repetitive patterns.

In China every cutter makes his or her own tools, which consist of knives of various sizes and shapes, and punches and chisels which are adapted to the particular work in hand. Handles made of two pieces of split bamboo are tied to metal pieces somewhat like small razor blades. They are shaped differently for cutting short or long lines, punching out small circles or triangles. The blades are sharpened constantly.

The papers to be cut are placed in a wooden box frame. The bottom is covered with a mixture of fat and charcoal which traditionally includes beeswax, although paraffin or other substances can be substituted. Once hardened, the cutting surface lasts for years and helps keep knives from being blunted. Before proceeding with cutting each new batch, the craftsperson scrapes the cutting surface clean and dusts it with flour so that the papers can be removed easily later on. The pile may consist of 10, 20, or even 50 sheets of paper, which are stacked on the base and topped by a pattern, all held in place with nails or large stitches.

Great experience and skill are required to drive the tools straight down to ensure that the bottom sheet does not vary from the pattern. Parts which have been cut away are removed with a pin.

The fineness of the work and the speed with which it is performed are truly amazing.

On completion, individual cuts are placed between sheets of paper for commercial distribution, but crafters who sell directly to consumers may keep their work in piles and peel off the required numbers of cuts when a customer makes a purchase.

Knife cuts are usually produced in sets of four, six, or eight figures related to one subject. A series may consist of birds and flowers, or children performing Wushu exercises, or a legend.

Knife cutting requires tissue paper, but the standard Chinese quality is somewhat more substantial than the gift wrapping tissue we are accustomed to using. Professional papercutters may cut freehand without drawings or use patterns which are made from strong paper so that they can be used over and over again. An original pattern is often sketched with a calligraphy brush and ink. The designer has to keep in mind that all parts of a papercut must be connected. Over the years Chinese cutters have cleverly developed links which appear as integral parts of the picture.

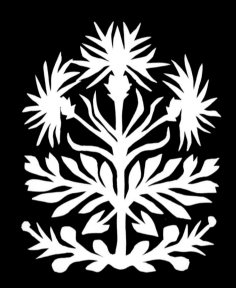

PAPERCUTS BY MRS. E.M. POSTHUMUS-KAMPMAN

actual size

THE NETHERLANDS, 20TH C.

Collection of Mingei International

PAPERCUTS

by Christian Schwizgebel

SWITZERLAND, 20TH C.

Collection of Mingei International

CUT PAPER STENCILS

for Stencil dying

Collection of Mingei International
Photograph by Allyson P. Kneib

84

9¾″H

MEXICO, 20TH C.

Collection of Jim and Veralee Bassler
Photograph by Allyson P. Kneib

PAPERCUT — MEXICO, 20TH C.

KITES

Dyed paper

INDIA, Contemporary

Collection of Mingei International
86   Photograph by Jim Coit

KITE—DYED PAPER

19½ʺ Diameter

INDIA, 20TH C.

Collection of Mingei International

Photograph by Jim Coit

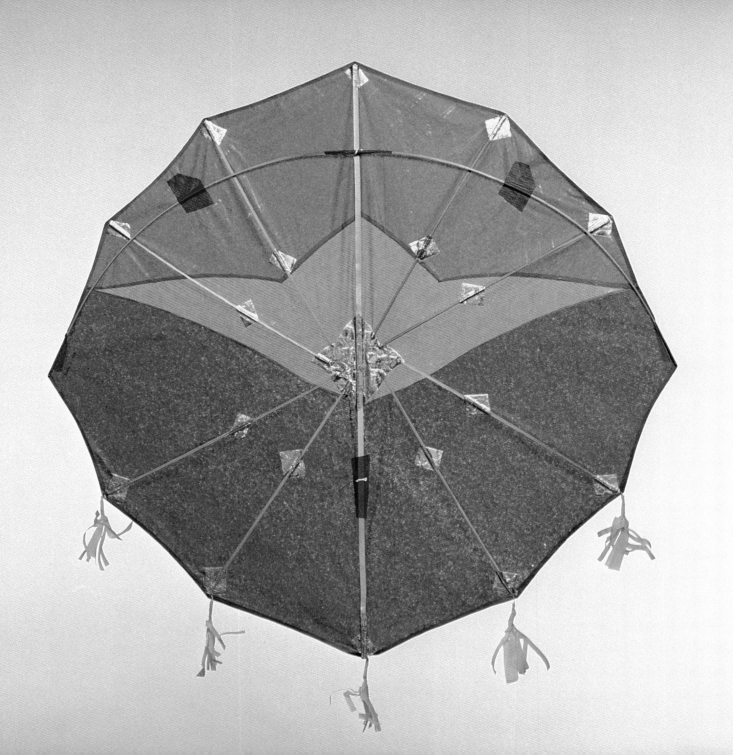

KITE

29″H x 22½″W

THAILAND, 20TH C.

90   Photograph by Jim Coit

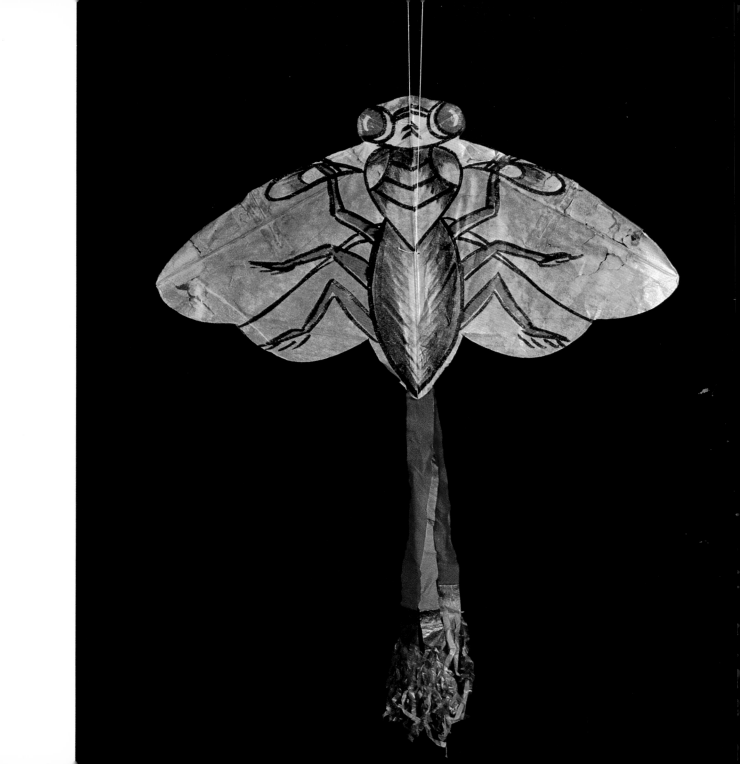

MINIATURE KITE

4⅞"H x 6½"W

JAPAN, Contemporary

Collection of Dinesh Bahadur

Photograph by Jim Coit

PHEASANT KITE

36½ ″H x 36″W x 3½ ″D   (Full sheet)

CHINA, Contemporary

Collection of Mingei International

Photograph by Carlos Richardson

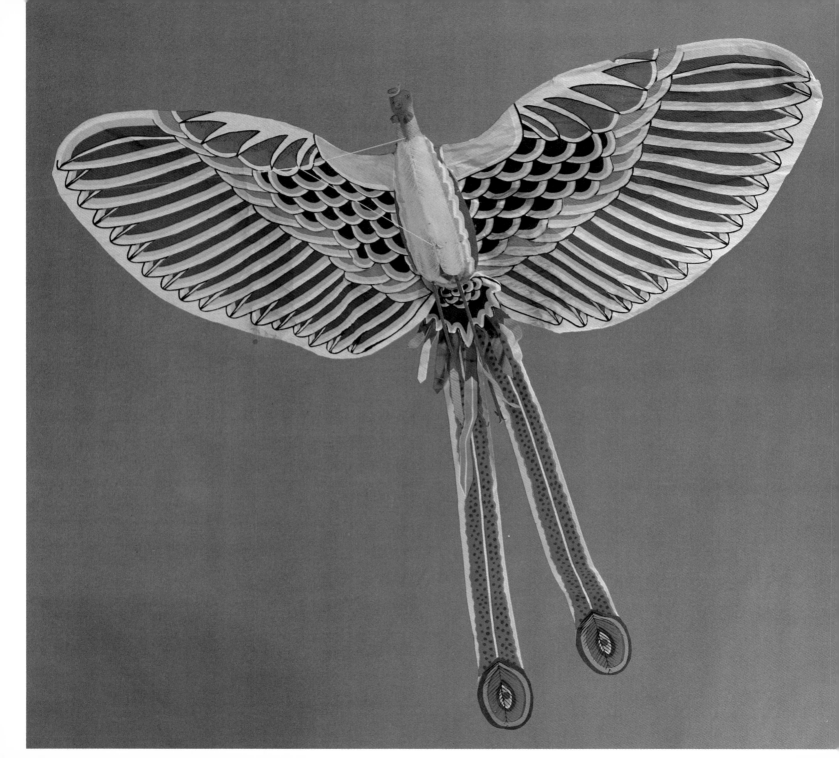

BOY'S DAY FISH WINDSOCK

32"H x 53"W

JAPAN Contemporary

Collection of Mingei International

Photograph by Allyson P. Kneib

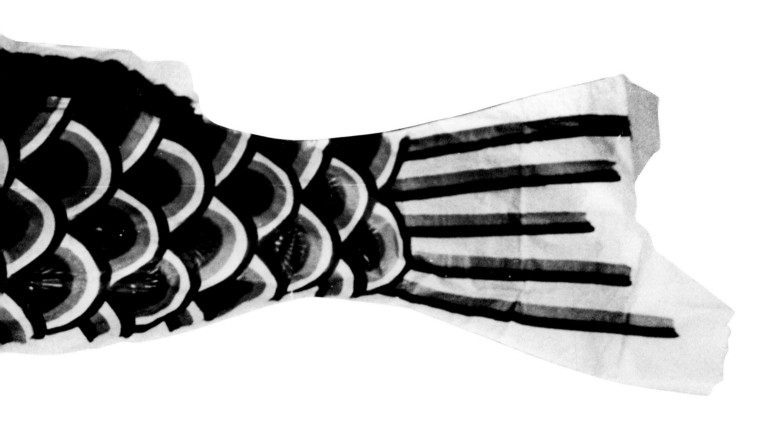

97

MARBELIZED PAPER

19½″ x 22½″   (Section of full sheet)

FRANCE, 20TH C.

Collection of Mingei International

Photograph by Jim Coit

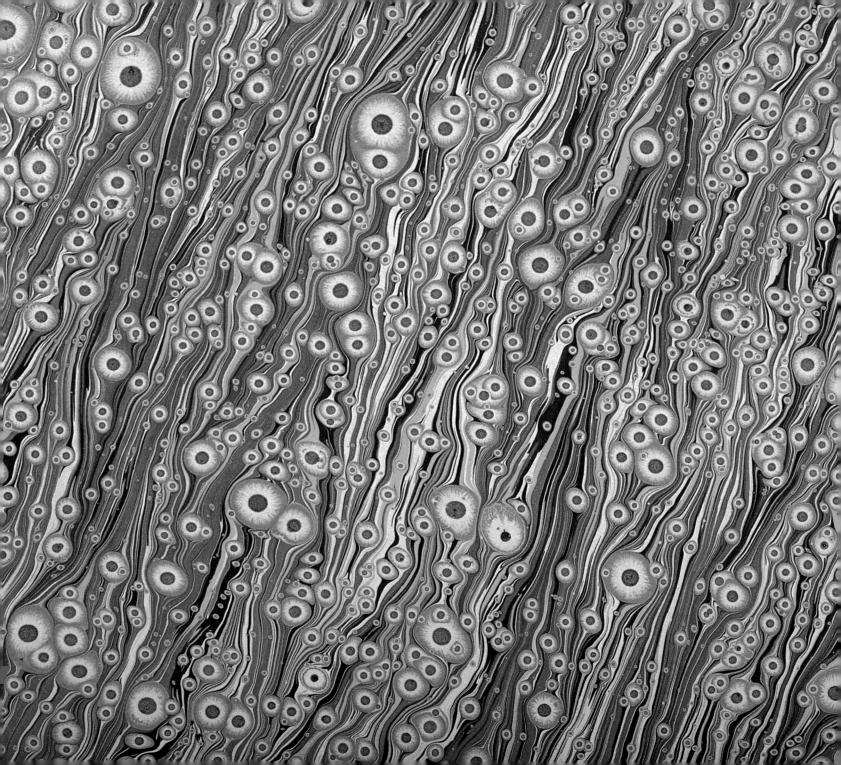

MARBELIZED PAPER

18 1/2 " x 27 "   (Full sheet)

ITALY, 20TH C.

100   Photograph by Jim Coit

POUPARD DOLL—PAPIER MACHÉ

12″H x 4¼″W x 3¼″D

FRANCE, 19TH C.

Collection of Joyce Malcolm

Photograph by Jim Coit

POUPARD DOLL—PAPIER MACHÉ

18½″H x 7½″W x 7¾″D

FRANCE, 19TH C.

Collection of Joyce Malcolm

Photograph by Jim Coit

PAPIER MACHÉ DOLL

BURMA, Contemporary

Photograph by Allyson P. Kneib

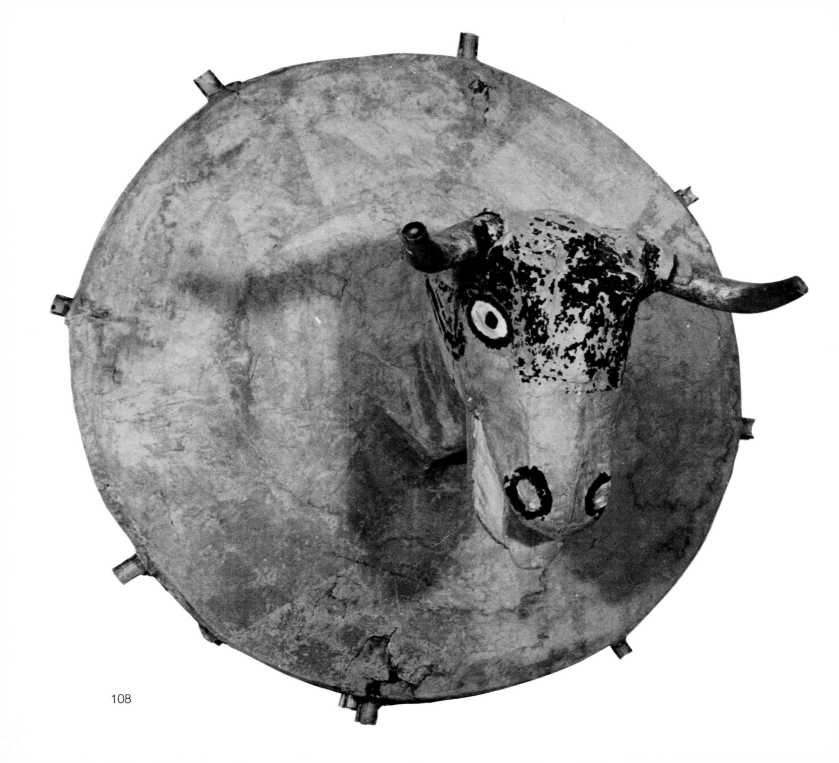

108

BULL'S HEAD—PAPIER MACHÉ

Advertisement for a shop which makes fireworks
33″ diameter 19″D

OCOTLAN, OAXACA, 20TH C.

Collection of Jim and Veralee Bassler
Photograph by Allyson P. Kneib

PIÑATA—PAPIER MACHÉ FIGURE
IN DRESS OF DYED TISSUE PAPER

33″H x 20″W x 6½″D

MEXICO, Contemporary

Collection of Mingei International
Photograph by Jim Coit

BRIDAL COUPLE

Cloth decorated with paper

INDIA, Contemporary

110   Photograph by Susan Sharp

DRAGON—PAPIER MACHÉ

26½ ″H

MEXICO, Contemporary

Collection of Rudy Vaca

Photograph by Jim Coit

LUZBEL OF PASTOREL—PAPIER MACHÉ PAINTED MASK

9½ "H x 8½ "W x 5½ "D

GUANAJUATO, MEXICO, 19TH C.

Collection of Pan American Museum Foundation

Photograph by Jim Coit

VASE—PAPIER MACHÉ

18½"H x 11" Diameter

KASHMIR, INDIA, Contemporary

Collection of Mingei International

ELEPHANT HEAD—PAPIER MACHÉ

25"H x 27"W x 23"D

INDIA, 20TH C.

Collection of Beatrice Wood

Photograph by Jim Coit

COW—PAPIER MACHÉ

7¾″H x 12½″W x 4½″D

JAPAN, 20TH C.

120   Photograph by Allyson P. Kneib

ACKNOWLEDGEMENT OF LENDERS

American Craft Museum
Dinesh Bahadur
Jim & Veralee Bassler
Dr. Robert Bishop, director
   Museum of American Folk Art, N.Y.
Mr. and Mrs. George Brosius
Martha Chatelain
China Books & Periodicals
Anne Dougal
Virginia Evans
Friends of Origami Center, N.Y.
Sukey Hughes
Korean Cultural Service
Japan House Gallery, Japan Society
Jean & Ernest W. Hahn
Isamu Kawaguchi
Martha Longenecker
Betty McKinstry
Joyce Malcolm
Fred & Barbara Meiers
Dorothy Miller
Hiroko Noguchi
Susan Olsen
Pan American Museum Foundation
Dinesh Pahadur
Dr. Ragab, The Papyrus Museum, Egypt
Sydney Martin Roth
Margaret Ahrens Sahlstrand
Sadako Sakurai
Amaury Saint Gilles
Jean & Mary Swiggett
Florence Temko
Rudy Vaca
Mitzie Verne
Beatrice Wood
Yamane Washi Shiryokan, Japan

Origami

David Brill
Steven Casey
Geric Drago
Robert Lang
Yoshihide Momotani
Emanuel Mooser
Asako Morita
Tibor Pataki
David Schall
Lore Schirokauer
Toshie Takahama
Arnold Tubis
Martin Wall
Steven Weiss
Akira Yoshizawa
   and students

MASK—PAPIER MACHÉ

7″W x 5″W x 2″D

JAPAN, Contemporary

Collection of Martha Longenecker
Photograph by Allyson P. Kneib

MINGEI INTERNATIONAL MUSEUM

Staff

MARTHA LONGENECKER, Director

MAUREEN KING, Director of Development

LESLIE B. BOUFFARD, Administrative Assistant

ELIZABETH PAYNE, Bookkeeper

NAN DANNINGER, Program Coordinator
Mgr. Collectors Gallery

TONY RACZKA, Registrar

PATRICIA BROWNING, Operations Assistant

PEGGY TRADER, Librarian

BETTY GRENSTED, Librarian

CONNIE STENGEL, Docent/Education

FRANCES ARMSTRONG, Membership Coordinator

SUSAN EYER, Membership Coordinator

EILEEN MILLER, Volunteer Coordinator

Legal Counsel   SHIRLEY KOVAR, Gary, Cary, Ames & Frye

Management Consultant   SYDNEY MARTIN ROTH

C.P.A.   BRUCE HEAP, Hutchinson & Bloodgood, C.P.A.

Exhibition

MARTHA LONGENECKER, designer

JOANNE HEANEY, co-designer

FLORENCE TEMKO, consultant

MARTHA CHATELAIN, consultant

STAFF & THE VOLUNTEER COUNCIL, installation

HUNTON SELLMAN, lighting

CLARISSA BEERBOWER, floral arrangements

HELENKA OSBORN, floral arrangements

EILEEN MILLER, reception chairman

Publication

MARTHA LONGENECKER–Design & Editing

COLOR GRAPHICS, Color Separations-John Luko

MOOG & ASSOCIATES, INC., Typesetting-Arlene Machado

VANARD LITHOGRAPHY, Printing

CHAMPION INTERNATIONAL CORPORATION, Paper
Cover, 12 pt Kromekote cover CIS
Text pages, 100 lb. Wedgewood Offset
End sheets, 70 lb. Carnival Groove–Sunshine

MINGEI INTERNATIONAL, incorporated in 1974, is a nonprofit public foundation dedicated to furthering the understanding of World Folk Arts. These are essential arts of people living in all times throughout the world which share in common a direct simplicity and joy in making, by hand, articles both useful and satisfying to the human spirit.

MINGEI INTERNATIONAL-MUSEUM OF WORLD FOLK ART was established May 5, 1978 as a unique center where "arts of the people" from all parts of the world speak directly for themselves of the rich diversity of individuals and cultures which are the roots of America.

Through the universal language of the line, form, and color, the "arts of the people" inspire appreciation of the similarities and distinctions of individuals and cultures.

MINGEI INTERNATIONAL'S ACTIVITIES are locating, collecting and documenting historical and contemporary world folk art which is used in specialized exhibitions and documentary publications of broad, universal and timely interest. Three to four major exhibitions are presented each year. Exhibitions are accompanied by authentic folk music, illustrated lectures, film, television programs and other educational events.

MINGEI INTERNATIONAL MUSEUM maintains a growing Permanent Collection of International Folk Art.

An additional research facility for members is the Museum's International Folk Art Reference Library of books, slides, films, videotapes and records.

MINGEI INTERNATIONAL MUSEUM is supported by memberships, volunteer services, and tax-exempt contributions (I.R.S. Section 501 c3). Membership is open to those who share interest in the museum's dedication.

MINGEI IS A SPECIAL TRANSCULTURAL WORD meaning "arts of the people" combining the Japanese words for people (min) and art (gei).

It was coined over fifty years ago by the late Dr. Soetsu Yanagi, revered scholar of Japan. His keen eye observed that many articles made by unknown craftsmen of pre-industrialized times were of a beauty seldom equaled by artists of modern societies. His questioning of why this might be revealed insight regarding the nature of beauty of things which are integrally related to life and born of a state of mind not attached to a conscious idea of beauty or ugliness. He realized that in the contemporary world of increasing mechanization and fragmentation of activities, more and more people seldom perform an act of total attention and that unsurpassed beauty is the natural flowering of a unified expression when there is no division of the craftsmen's head, heart and hands.

In his desire to communicate this profound insight, Dr. Yanagi, together with the potters Shoji Hamada and Kanjiro Kawai, founded the Mingei Association and first Folk Art Museum in Japan.

Many of the contemporary craftsmen whom Yanagi nurtured became designated as Living National Treasures of Japan. Their work possesses qualities of naturaliness and beauty akin to that of the unknown craftsmen of prior days.

Thus the Japanese heritage of "arts of the people" was not lost to the present and future generations as is happening throughout the industrialized world. The understanding of the world significance and influence of Mingei has been conveyed through the writings of the late English potter and author, Bernard Leach in *The Unknown Craftsman and Hamada*.

Inspired by but not officially connected with the Mingei Association of Japan, MINGEI INTERNATIONAL-MUSEUM OF WORLD FOLK ART was established in University Towne Centre, San Diego, to bring the arts of the people from all parts of the world "to the people" so that they may come to see, discover, know and enjoy.

GANESHA —PAPIER MACHÉ

14½ "H x 12"W x 2½ "D

INDIA, 20TH C.

Collection of Beatrice Wood
Photograph by Jim Coit

127

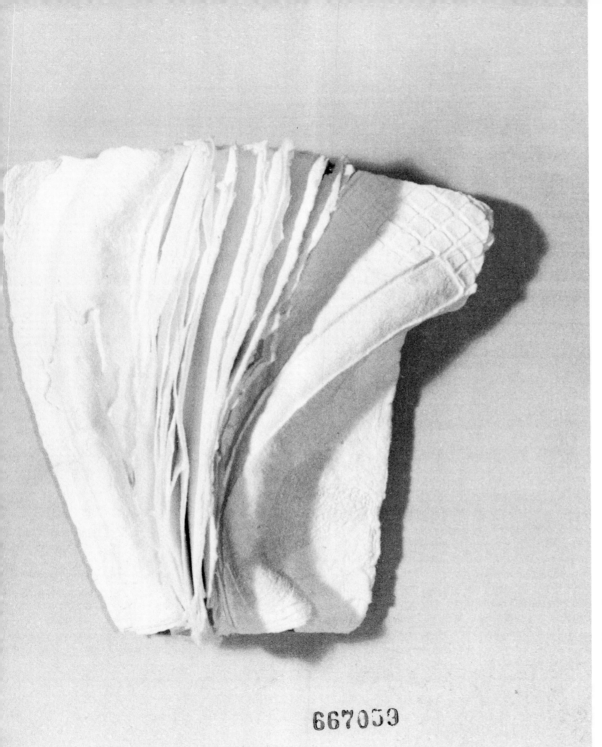

667053

SHIRO SHIRO—
MADE BY MARTHA CHATELAIN

Handmade Formed Paper

12″H x 10¾″W x 2⅛″D

UNITED STATES

Collection of the artist

GOLD-FOIL CUT-PAPER MOURNING PICTURE

16″H x 20″W

UNITED STATES (Pennsylvania) c. 1850

Collection of Robert Bishop, Director American Folk Art Museum, N.Y.

2 Photograph by Schecter Lee

"To be classified as true paper the thin sheets must be made from fiber that has been macerated until each individual filament is a separate unit, the fibres lifted from the water in the form of a thin stratum, the water draining through the small openings of the screen, leaving a sheet of matted fribre upon the screen's surface. This thin layer of intertwined fibre is paper, and in our own time the most ponderous and most eficient papermaking machine employs precisely this same principle. The actual fibre formation of paper has undergone no change in almost 7,000 years."

Papermaking, The History and Techniques of the Ancient Craft by Dard Hunter